WELCOME TO MELROSE ABBEY

Melrose Abbey, in the heart of the beautiful Scottish Border country, was founded in the twelfth century by the Cistercian order of monks. They were drawn to this fertile spot beside the River Tweed through its intimate associations with the holy men St Aidan and St Cuthbert. The abbey grew to become one of the wealthiest and most majestic medieval monasteries in Scotland, and its abbey church is one of the finest expressions of the order's 'architecture of solitude'.

Melrose Abbey no longer sits in solitude but in a busy Border town. Within a radius of just a few miles lie the splendid ruins of the three other great Border abbeys – Kelso, Jedburgh and Dryburgh. Together they form the greatest concentration of medieval religious houses in Scotland.

Above: The effigy of St Mary the Virgin cradling the infant Jesus, on the exterior of the abbey church, named in her honour.

CONTENTS

Left: The graceful ruined abbey church of St Mary the Virgin, Melrose, with the River Tweed in the distance.

MELROSE ABBEY AT A GLANCE

From the time of its foundation in 1136 down to the day the last monk died in 1590, the great abbey church of St Mary the Virgin at Melrose loomed large in the lives of many, on both sides of the border with England. The great and good richly endowed it, and a hallowed few were privileged to be buried there; they included Alexander II (died 1249) and Robert the Bruce (died 1329).

Such was the fame and importance of Melrose that it attracted unwanted attention from the English during the long and bitter Wars of Independence. The present rose-stoned abbey church dates almost entirely from a rebuilding following a devastating raid by Richard II's army in 1385, and is regarded as one of the marvels of medieval church architecture to be seen anywhere in the British Isles.

Right: The town of Melrose; painted by I Clark in 1825. The new parish church, built on the Weirhill in 1810, is visible just to the right of the ancient abbey.

HOLY MEN

28 ST CUTHBERT
This towering figure of the early church began his monastic career at 'Old Melrose'.

32 KING DAVID I
The founder of Melrose Abbey was known as 'a sair [sore] saint for the croun' because of the money he lavished on building and endowing monasteries.

32 ST WALTHEOF
Miracles performed at the tomb of the second abbot helped put Melrose on the pilgrimage map.

A FEAST OF SCULPTURE

12 STATUES
Fascinating stone figures still grace the inside walls of the church, despite the unwelcome attentions of the Protestant Reformers.

16 THE BAGPIPE PLAYING PIG
Undoubtedly most people's favourite sculpture.

19 ANGELS AND DEVILS
Demons and hobgoblins vie with lute-playing angels for space on the outside walls of the church.

OBJECTS OF EVERYDAY LIFE

ROYAL MAUSOLEUM

20 URINALS
Found in the main drain that flushed the monks' toilets.

25 COOKING POTS
Discovered in the main drain near the site of the refectory.

39 COMMUNION TOKEN
Left behind by one of the post-Reformation parishioners.

32 KING ALEXANDER II
Died in 1249 in far-off Argyll, whilst fighting the Norwegians, but was buried at Melrose.

35 KING ROBERT THE BRUCE
His body was buried at Dunfermline Abbey in 1329, but his heart was interred at Melrose in 1331.

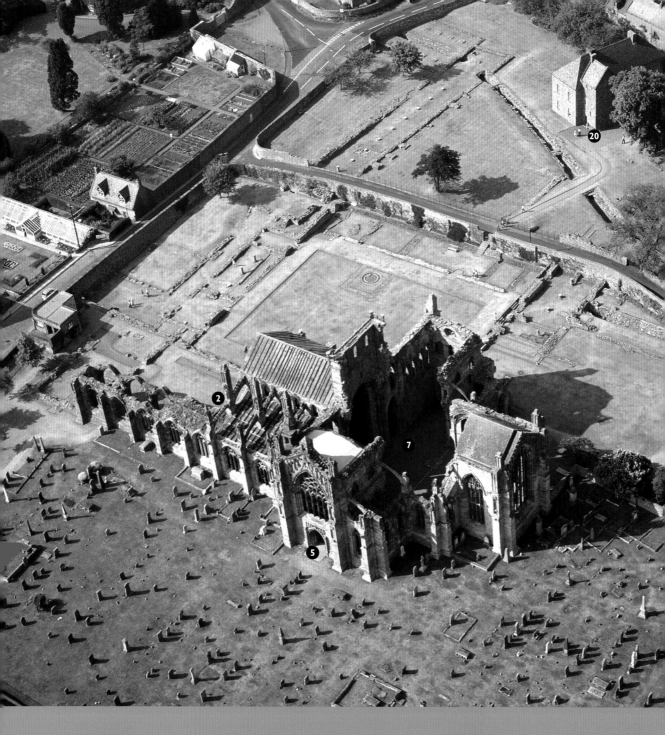

A GUIDED TOUR

This tour guides the visitor around the abbey, pointing out the features of interest. It begins with the impressive abbey church, which, despite its chequered history, is the best-preserved part of the entire complex, then progresses around the cloister, ending in the commendator's house, with its fascinating displays of objects found at the abbey.

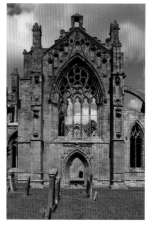

Above: The south transept.

Opposite page top: An aerial view of Melrose Abbey from the south-east.

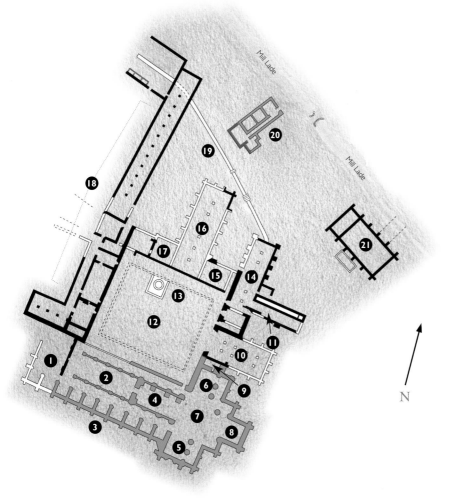

N

Plan key

1	Porch	8	Presbytery	15	Warming room
2	Nave	9	Sacristy	16	Refectory
3	Aisle chapels	10	Chapter house	17	Kitchen
4	Monks' choir	11	Latrine	18	Lay brothers' range
5	South transept	12	Cloister	19	Main drain
6	North transept	13	Wash place	20	Commendator's house
7	Crossing	14	Novices' day room	21	Abbot's hall

■ 12th - 13th century
▧ 1385 - 1590
▦ 1618
■ Modern

THE ABBEY CHURCH

The original church, erected in the twelfth century, was largely destroyed by Richard II's English army in 1385. The structure which replaced it is the magnificent building we see today.

On plan the surviving church resembled the earlier building but on a bigger scale. The transepts and presbytery were enlarged and extended further to the east and a series of chapels was built opening off the south aisle of the nave. The contemplated west end was never completed and the original front was never entirely demolished.

Below: Melrose Abbey church looking along the nave from the west.

1 Nave
2 Original west wall (12th century)
3 'Galilee' porch
4 South aisle
5 Aisle chapels
6 Screen

THE NAVE

The western part of the nave was for the exclusive use of the lay brothers for their church services. With the disappearance of lay brothers from the order in the fifteenth century, the need to complete the nave became less urgent.

The only part of the first church surviving is the fragment of the west wall with the lower part of the entrance doorway, the foundations of the square nave piers and their connecting screen-walls, and the meagre remains of part of the north wall.

The original west front had a 'Galilee' porch added on its outer, west side in the thirteenth century. There the Sunday procession was assembled. Within it is a number of burials, the fragmentary grave-covers of which still remain. Entered off the south aisle of the nave is a series of side chapels.

THE SCREEN – *pulpitum*

At the east end of the nave is a stone screen, called the *pulpitum*, which separated the lay brothers' choir from the monks' choir to the east. The upper part has been destroyed, but the beautiful cornice remains. To the south of the central doorway is a wall-cupboard for holding furnishings used at the lay brothers' altars. Within the short passage is a ceiling boss bearing the head of Christ, and on the north side a small stair once led to the loft.

Below:

1 The graceful stone vaulting over one of the aisle chapels.

2 The carved head of Christ in the *pulpitum*.

5

7

THE AISLE CHAPELS

Eight aisle chapels survive. The three western chapels were the last to be completed, in the time of Abbot William Turnbull (1503–06).

Each chapel was entered through a doorway in a wooden screen which separated the chapel from the aisle. Altars with decorative altar pieces, or retables, above stood against the east walls. The basins, or *piscinae*, in which the altar vessels were rinsed, are in the south wall. The insides of the bowls are either scalloped or plain and the outside ornamentation is of leaf pattern. On either side of most of the *piscinae* are niches which held the altar cruets during the Eucharist.

In the third chapel from the west Abbot Turnbull's initials can faintly be seen on the back wall of the *piscina*. A grave-slab against the south wall once bore a figure of a man and an inscription 'Here lies an honourable man George Haliburton (who died 1 October 1538)'.

The fourth chapel may have been dedicated to St Michael, as his image can be seen in the central boss of the vaulting. Another boss is carved with an angel holding a shield on which are seen the decayed arms of Abbot Andrew Hunter (1444–65). The grave-slabs show that this chapel became the burial-place of the Pringles of Woodhouse and Whytebank.

The fifth chapel became the burial-place of the Scotts, lairds of Gala, and the Pringles of Galashiels, and contains a crude effigy of Andrew Pringle, who resided at Smailholm Tower and died in 1585.

The three chapels furthest east were used as part of the post-Reformation parish kirk and the joist holes for the inserted galleries are still visible. The sixth chapel has a monument to David Fletcher, who was minister of Melrose before becoming bishop of Argyll. He died in 1665.

Set into the floor of the eighth chapel is a thirteenth-century tomb, of prayer-desk form. The inscription on the sloping top reads ORATE PRO/ANIMA FRATRIS PETRI CEL[L]ARII ('Pray for the soul of Brother Peter, the cellarer').

Above: Flowing tracery window in an aisle chapel.

Below: A monk at prayer in an aisle chapel c1500.

Right: A basin, *piscina*, in one of the aisle chapels, with its beautifully carved canopy and scalloped bowl.

HEIR LIES ANE HO/NORA[BIL VO]MAN CRISTIN LVNDIE / SPOVS TO IAM[ES PRINGIL OF] QVHYTBANK SCHO DECEIS/SIT 19 JVLY 1602 / LAMENT FOR / SYN AND STYL THOV MVRN / FOR TO THE CL/AY [ALL] VE MEN TVRN.

'Here lies an honourable woman, Christine Lundie, spouse to James Pringle of Whytebank, who deceased 19 July 1602. Lament for that time and still thou mourn, for to the clay all ye must turn.'

Above: Christine Lundie's epitaph in the fourth aisle chapel, appropriated by the Pringles of Whytebank as their burial vault after the Reformation (1560).

THE MONKS' CHOIR

The monks' choir occupied the space between the *pulpitum* and the presbytery, and their choir-stalls were set against the screens which separated the choir from the aisles. The pier-caps here are beautifully arranged and carved with leaf ornament.

The monks' choir was adapted for use as a parish church in the early seventeenth century. The rib vaulting was removed and the inner arcades of the south clearstory windows were lowered and altered. Massive stone piers were built up against the north arcade to carry a plain stone vault, and walls with windows were erected at either end. The interior was fitted out with galleries. The erection of a new parish church elsewhere in the town in 1810 resulted in this kirk being abandoned and the end walls taken down, leaving the structure as it appears today, a dismal tunnel masking the beautiful proportions and designs of the fifteenth-century church.

Opposite page: An artist's impression of the monks at service in their choir c1500.

Left: Monks' choir details.

1 A pier in the monks' choir with its elegant lines and attractive leaf-decoration.

2 The present massive stone piers and ugly stone vault, inserted c1610 to form a parish kirk, utterly despoiled the splendour of this medieval creation.

THE TRANSEPTS

T he two transepts on either side of the central crossing housed additional altars in the eastern chapels where the monks offered up private prayers for the souls of their patrons. Each chapel had an altar under the east window.

The north transept chapels were dedicated to St Peter and St Paul; their statues stand in canopied niches high up on the west wall of the transept. The chapels flanking the presbytery were dedicated to St Benedict (north) and possibly St Martin (south). The dedications of the south transept chapels are not known.

In the north-west corner of the north transept, a wide stone stair once led through the round-headed doorway to the monks' dormitory. This was the 'night-stair', used by the monks when going to and from their night services. Beside the first step is a holy-water stoup where the brethren ritually washed their hands before entering the church. In the centre of the north wall is the doorway into the sacristy, where the altar vestments and other church items were kept; it was described as a 'wax cellar' in 1558. High above the doorway is a long, sunken panel which was probably decorated with images of metal or wood set on the 14 large and 14 small stone pedestals. Above this are three arched openings into the clearstory passage, and over all is a circular window with its tracery still complete.

In the west wall of the south transept are two interesting inscriptions. Both refer to a Parisian born master-mason John Morow who was responsible for the fine detailing of the south transept windows and for the earliest of the chapels along the south side of the nave. He was active around 1400. They read:

'John Morow sometimes called was I and born in Paris certainly and had in keeping all the mason work of St Andrews, the high kirk of Glasgow, Melrose and Paisley, of Nithsdale and Galloway. I pray to God and Mary both and sweet St John to keep this holy church from harm' and 'As the compass goes evenly about, so truth and loyalty shall do without doubt. Look to the end quoth John Morow.'

Above: St Peter with key and books high up on the west wall of the north transept.

Right: The north transept.

Above: John Morow's inscription in the south transept reads:

[IOHN MOROW SUM
TY]M CALLIT [WAS I
AND BORN] IN PARYSSE/
[CERTANLY AND HAD]
IN KEPYING/ [AL MASON
WERK] OF SANTAN/
[DROYS YE HYE K]YRK
OF GLAS/ [GW MELROS
AND] PASLAY OF/
[NYDDYSDAYLL AND OF]
GALWAY/ [I PRAY TO GOD
AND MAR]I BATHE/
[& SWETE SANCT IOHNE
TO KEPE/ THIS HALY
KYRK FRA SKATHE].

THE PRESBYTERY

The presbytery housed the high altar. It was lit by a magnificent 'perpendicular' window in the east wall and fine windows to the south and north. Under the east window are two wall-cupboards, and in the south wall a credence, or small table for the sacraments, and a double *piscina*. Under the side windows are recesses for tombs. Although it had originally been forbidden for laymen to be buried within Cistercian churches, the rule was relaxed and the presbytery became the burial place for the elite in society; Bishop Bondington of Glasgow was interred here in 1258 and Alexander II in 1249. Robert the Bruce's heart was also probably laid to rest here in 1331.

Above: The presbytery; painted by F J Sarjent in 1811.

Above

An intricate pattern of ribs and bosses adorns the vaulted ceiling of the presbytery. The central boss, positioned directly over the high altar, is a representation of the Holy Trinity attended by two angels. To the west is St Andrew holding his cross, and reading clockwise are: St Bartholomew holding the flaying knife, St Peter with the keys, St Thomas with the spear, St James the Less grasping the bludgeon, St James the Greater holding his staff and a scrip or costrel, St Paul with a sword, and St Matthias with an axe. To the south of St Andrew is a saint holding a book. Another boss has an angel and other bosses are carved with roses and leaves.

THE EXTERIOR OF THE CHURCH

The doorway in the south transept leads to the graveyard on the south side of the abbey church. This was the final resting-place for the monks before becoming the parish burial ground. The best views of the magnificent church are to be had from there.

The exterior was lavishly enriched with sculptural decoration, and although much of the statuary is missing, what survives is still one of the most accomplished collections of medieval carving surviving in Scotland. There are gargoyles shaped like strange animals or flying dragons that belched out the roof-water, an array of demons, devils and hobgoblins on the buttresses and gables, beautiful images of Christ, the Virgin Mary, saints and martyrs in the elaborate niches, angel musicians on the projecting corbels, and heads of kings, queens, lords, ladies, monks, craftsmen and crones smirking, smiling, growling and grimacing down from their places around the windows.

THE AISLE CHAPELS

Amongst the decoration on the buttresses supporting the aisle chapels is a shield bearing the royal arms of James IV, dated 1505. Under the shield is another shield which once displayed the arms of Abbot William Turnbull, and on either side a mell, or mason's mallet, and a rose – a rebus on the name Melrose. This play on words is repeated on an adjacent buttress.

Above: The elegant south transept's deeply recessed doorway. This part of the church may have been built in the early 1400s to designs by the Frenchman, John Morow, whose inscriptions are in the south transept (see page 12).

Below: External features to look out for.

1 The royal arms of James IV.

2 Melrose Abbey's famous bagpipe-playing pig.

3 The rebus (play on words) on the name Melrose, carved on a chapel buttress.

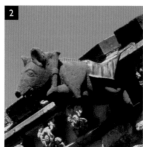

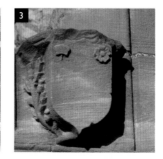

Set in an elaborate niche adorning the westernmost high buttress is a mutilated figure of the Virgin and Child (see page 1). The abbey church at Melrose, in common with all Cistercian houses, was dedicated to St Mary the Virgin, and it is appropriate that the position of this sculpture, in alignment with the *pulpitum,* marks externally the western limit of the monks' choir. The Virgin is defaced and the Child is headless. Nonetheless, the effigy is arguably the finest piece of medieval figure-sculpture surviving in Scotland. The Virgin is veiled and crowned and the drapery of her robes falls in well-balanced folds. The infant is held on her left arm and with the right hand she holds a flower. The canopy over the Virgin and the supporting corbel are also elaborately carved.

In the niche of the next high buttress is St Andrew, now very defaced. It was not designed to fit the niche and the statue may have been brought here from elsewhere in the church. At the wall-head of this part of the building are two charming gargoyles, or water-spouts; one depicts a winged, calf-headed beast, and the other a pig playing the bagpipes!

'In this fabric there are the finest lessons and the greatest variety of gothic ornaments that the island affords, take all the religious structures together.'

Frederick Pinches in
The Abbey Church of Melrose

Below: The abbey church from the south east, with the presbytery on the right and the south transept on the left.

THE SOUTH TRANSEPT

From the outside, the south transept forms a most attractive composition. The arrangement of the niches with their projecting canopies and carved corbels is exceptionally pleasing. The lower niche-corbels are carved with reclining figures of bearded men holding labels; the label of the figure on the west buttress is inscribed:

TIMET[E] DEU[M] ('fear the Lord'),
another has a scroll inscribed:

CU[M] VEN[IT] JES[US] SEQ[UAX?] CESSABIT [UMBRA]
('When Jesus comes the shadow will cease'),
and a third displays the words:

PASSUS E[ST] Q[UIA] IP[S]E VOLUIT
('He suffered because He himself willed it').

The doorway is deeply recessed and at the point of the arch is a shield with the royal arms. On either side is an array of images, now headless: St Andrew, St Peter, a kneeling figure with hands clasped, a kneeling figure holding a book, St Paul and St Thomas. Set a little above in the centre of the group is a bearded man holding a scroll with the words:

ECCE FILIUS DEI ('Behold the Son of God').

Immediately above the great window is an elaborate niche which probably contained a seated figure of the Virgin. The belfry at the top of the gable was built in 1618 for the post-Reformation kirk; the Dutch bell still survives with its inscription:

IAN BURGERHVYS ME FECIT 1608
('Ian Burgerhuys made me 1608').

Corbels on the walls of the eastern chapels represent a monk telling his beads, angels with curly hair and smiling faces and playing musical instruments, a cook with a ladle, and a mason with his chisel and mell.

THE PRESBYTERY

The east gable of the presbytery is renowned for its grace and symmetry. Above the window is a seated group representing the Coronation of the Virgin. On either side are statues; the one on the south side a mitred ecclesiastic. Quaint, cross-legged figures of men or women perch on the slopes of the buttresses.

Opposite Page: The graceful elevation of the south transept, designed by the French master-mason John Morow, together with a selection of sculptural ornament adorning this and other exterior elevations.

Above: The apex of the east gable. At the centre is the seated group representing the Coronation of the Virgin.

TIMET[E] DEU[M]

'Fear the Lord'

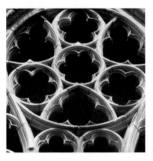

ECCE FILIUS DEI

'Behold the Son of God'

PASSUS E[ST] Q[UIA] IP[S]E VOLUIT

'He suffered because He himself willed it'

THE CONVENTUAL BUILDINGS

The monks' living quarters were on the north side of the abbey church. This was unusual, the preference being to place the cloister and conventual buildings on the south side where the towering height of the church would not shut out the sunshine. The decision to build on the north was probably made so that fresh running water from the Tweed could be easily diverted for the many uses required of it.

The conventual buildings are now largely represented by low stone walls, discovered during excavations. Only the commendator's house stands complete, albeit heavily restored. It was built in 1590 using stonework from the ruined cloister ranges. It now houses a display of objects found during excavations.

THE CLOISTER

The Cistercian Rule insisted that monks should spend their entire day within the church and enclosed world of the cloister. At the centre of the cloister was an open rectangular space, or garth, probably laid out as a garden.

Around the garth were four covered alleys which sheltered the monks as they passed from one building to another and where they worked. The surviving walls of the cloister, to either side of the east processional doorway into the church, have stone benches and elaborate wall arcades.

THE EAST RANGE

The east alley contained the most important rooms. Closest to their church was the chapter house, the main meeting room (see page 22), and beside it probably the inner parlour, where necessary conversation was permitted; for much of the time the brethren were sworn to silence. The end of the range was completed by a two-aisled undercroft of seven bays, probably the novices' day room, and to its east the lower part of the reredorter, or latrine block, serving the monks' dormitory, which ran the full length of the east range at first-floor level.

Right: The east cloister alley viewed from the east processional doorway.

Right inset: The east processional doorway into the church and part of the elaborate wall arcades and stone benches along the south alley; painted by Robert Billings in 1832.

Left: Ceramic urinals of fourteenth-century date found during excavation and on display in the commendator's house.

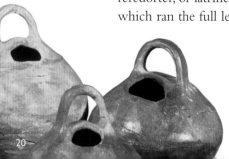

'The dwelling place of the convent was the cloister [which] as well as providing ample space for contemplative activities such as reading and instruction afforded easy and direct access to their buildings'.

Stewart Cruden *Scottish Abbeys* 1960

THE CHAPTER HOUSE

The chapter house was the main meeting room. There the monks met every morning, to hear a chapter of the Rule of St Benedict, to confess misdemeanours, and to discuss business matters. It was also a favoured place of burial for abbots and other church dignitaries. Perhaps the most important interment was that of St Waltheof in 1159.

In addition to ecclesiastical figures, the chapter house was the resting-place for patrons of the abbey. The *Melrose Chronicle* records numerous interments, including Philip de Valognes, William I's chamberlain, in 1215, and Christiana Corbet, a relation of the earl of Dunbar, in 1241. Was she perhaps the female skeleton found in a stone coffin in 1921?

Undoubtedly the most intriguing discovery in 1921 is of a mummified heart enclosed in a lead container. Decomposed iron box straps were found beside it, though nothing to indicate its history. It has been suggested that this was the heart of Robert the Bruce, interred at Melrose in 1331. This seems unlikely. Heart burial was quite common in the Middle Ages, and we know that Bruce's heart was laid to rest in the abbey church beside the high altar.

Above:

1 Stone coffins discovered beneath the floor of the chapter house in 1921.

2 The lead casket found in the chapter house in 1921, and again in 1996.

Left: Archaeological excavations underway in the chapter house in 1996, showing numerous stone coffins under the floor. The heart casket discovered in 1921, and thought to have been Robert the Bruce's heart, was found, examined and re-interred.

THE NORTH RANGE

The north alley housed the main domestic rooms, including the warming house, the only room where the monks were permitted to warm themselves, and then only for short periods each day. In the centre of the alley was the refectory, or dining hall, where the monks ate in silence.

The dining hall was originally built parallel to the north walk, but in the thirteenth century was rebuilt at right angles to it, probably to create a much larger space. The *lavatorium*, or wash place, directly opposite the refectory entrance was a great circular basin, fed with water brought in lead pipes from a well to the south of the abbey. To the west of the refectory was the kitchen.

THE LAY BROTHERS' RANGE

The lay brothers lived in their own cloister which lay to the west of the monks' cloister. The remains are mostly underneath the public road. The east range extended from the west porch of the church for a distance of 108 m (320 ft) and comprised two buildings. The north block was 14 bays long with a central line of pillars and at its south end was the refectory. A fireplace in the west wall indicates the site of the warming house. The south block may have started as the refectory, and later been converted into workshops. Three leather tanning pits survive.

Above:

1 The tanning pits in the lay brothers' range.

2 The main drain where most of the artefacts on display in the commendator's house were discovered.

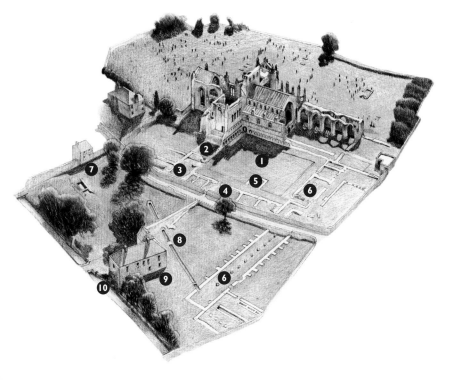

Plan key:

1 Cloister
2 Chapter house
3 Novices' day room
4 Dining hall
5 Wash place
6 Lay brothers' cloister
7 Abbot's hall
8 Main drain
9 Commendator's house
10 Mill-lade.

BEYOND THE CLOISTER

The *Melrose Chronicle* for 1246 records that Abbot Matthew erected a magnificent hall on the bank of the stream together with many convenient offices. The foundations of his hall, the abbot's hall, are probably those just south of the mill-lade.

The mill-lade is fed from a dam across the Tweed 460 m (1/4 mile) to the west of the abbey. Part of its function was to power the abbey's mills, but before it reached the westernmost abbey buildings, part of it was diverted and carried along a main drain, or sewer, to flush the latrines in the east range.

COMMENDATOR'S HOUSE

The commendator's house was originally built in the fifteenth century and contained at least three rooms on the ground floor, each with a hooded fireplace. The upper rooms were entered from a timber gallery extending along the east facade and reached by an outside stair at the north end. The function of the building is unknown. In 1590 James Douglas, the last commendator of the abbey, converted it into his house. The gallery was removed and the square stair-tower added at the corner. Vaulted cellars and a kitchen were inserted in the ground floor and the upper floors reorganised.

The building now houses one of the finest collections of objects and architectural fragments from any ecclesiastical site in Britain, most of them found in the main drain.

Left: The commendator's house from across the mill-lade.

Below

1 A variety of medieval pottery vessels found during excavation and on display in the commendator's house.

2 The inscribed lintel over the entrance into the commendator's house. The initials stand for James Douglas, the last commendator, and Mary Ker, his wife.

1

2

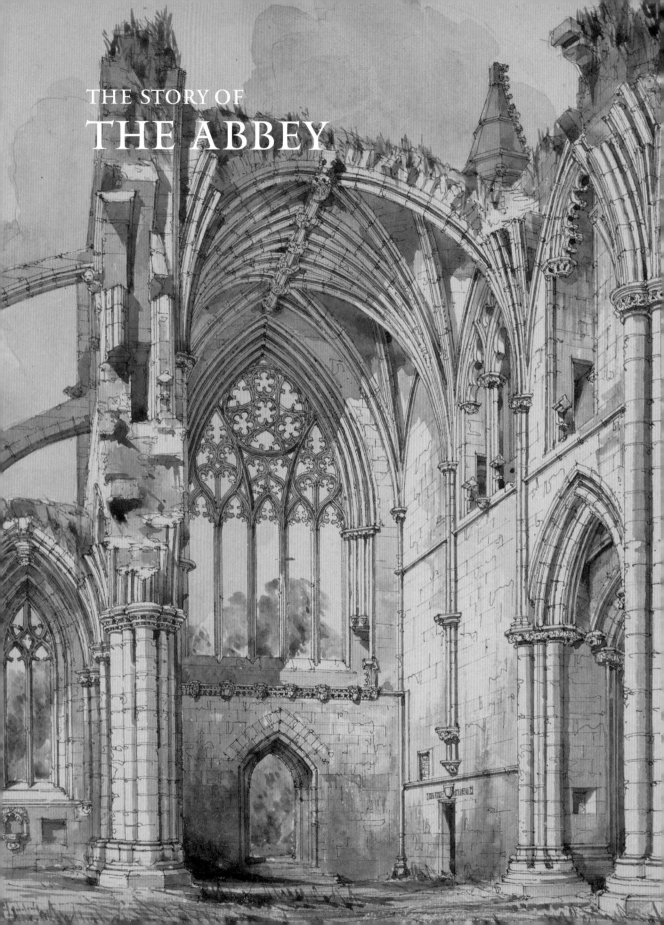

THE STORY OF
THE ABBEY

Melrose Abbey is arguably the finest of the Scottish Border abbeys and its story is a fascinating one. It begins deep in the Dark Ages with the arrival of Celtic monks to Old Melrose just 2.5 miles (4 km) to the east of the present abbey, continues with the advent of the Cistercians in 1136, who through their diligence and hard work created one of the richest and most magnificent abbeys in Scotland, and ends not at the Reformation in 1560 but in the early nineteenth century with the building of a new parish kirk elsewhere in the prosperous town of Melrose.

Melrose Abbey has associations with many famous historical figures, among them St Aidan, St Cuthbert and St Waltheof, David I and Robert the Bruce of Scotland and King Richard II of England.

'The abbey of St Mary of Melrose was founded on Monday, being the second day of Easter week [23 March] and its first abbot was Richard.'

An entry in the *Melrose Chronicle* for the year 1136

Opposite page: The elegant south transept; painted by Robert Billings in 1832.

1 Melrose Abbey from the east.

2 Melrose Abbey; painted by James Ward.

3 A rebus, or play on the word Melrose, which the monks adopted as their logo – a mel (stone-mason's mallet) and rose.

'OLD' MELROSE

A little to the east of Melrose, beside the winding River Tweed, is a secluded spot called Old Melrose. It is here that Melrose's story truly begins shortly before the year 650. It was at this time that St Aidan of Lindisfarne established a monastery here, 'Mailros', bringing monks from the Columban monastery on Iona. Mailros then lay within the Anglian kingdom of Northumbria, and its first abbot, Eata, was one of 12 Saxon youths taught by Aidan. The first prior, St Boisil, a quiet and unassuming monk, gave his name to the village of St Boswells, and another monk, St Bothan, is remembered in the nearby village of Bowden.

Old Melrose's most famous son was St Cuthbert. A Borderer by birth, Cuthbert entered the monastery following a vision whilst shepherding on the Lammermuir Hills, apparently on the very night St Aidan died in 651. The young lad, who loved games and pranks, in time succeeded Boisil as prior of Old Melrose and in 664 became prior of Lindisfarne. Two centuries later Old Melrose was no more. The abbey that Cuthbert knew had been destroyed by the Scots. But the sanctity of the place lived on, and between 1073-5 it served as a retreat for Prior Turgot of Durham, later confessor and chronicler to St Margaret of Scotland.

'Now he (St Cuthbert) entered first the monastery of Melrose which is enclosed for the most part by a loop of the river tweed, and which was then ruled by its abbot, eata, the most meek and simple of all men.'

The Venerable Bede (d. 735), in his *Life of Saint Cuthbert*

Above: The River Tweed and Melrose from Scott's View, painted by J M W Turner for Sir Walter Scott's *Poetical Works* (1832). This panorama, looking west over Old Melrose towards the abbey and town of Melrose and the Eildon Hills beyond, was Scott's favourite view. Scott is pictured sitting in the foreground.

Left: The lid of St Cuthbert's coffin, carved with the figure of Christ.

Little is known of the planning of these early monasteries, but at Old Melrose at least the boundary is visible, a ditch, *vallum*, cutting off the neck of the promontory on which the monastery stood. At the heart of the monastery was the church and around it the individual cells or huts of the monks, their granaries, storehouses, workshops and guestrooms.

When St Margaret's youngest son, David I, invited the Cistercian monks from Rievaulx to set up their first house in Scotland, he chose Old Melrose. The monks seem not to have found the site to their liking and opted for a spot a little further west called Little Fordell, now Melrose itself. A church of sorts, however, did continue at Old Melrose for at least another century.

Above: The site of Old Melrose lies within a winding of the River Tweed. In the distance are the three peaks of the Eildon Hills (*Trimontium*) and to their right the town of Melrose with its abbey. The photograph was taken from Scott's View.

651

ST CUTHBERT
a humble shepherd boy, enrols as a monk at Old Melrose. Leaves in 664 to become prior of Lindisfarne.

850

SCOTS CONQUER
the borders from the Anglians of Northumbria possibly under their King, Kenneth MacAlpin (right). They destroy Old Melrose in the by-going.

THE CISTERCIANS

The Cistercian movement was established in 1098 at Citeaux, near Dijon, by monks from the Cluniac house at Molesme. It was one of numerous attempts to return a degenerate monastic system to the strict Rule of St Benedict. The rise of the order was meteoric despite its uncompromising insistence on poverty and labour. The first Cistercian house founded in Britain was Waverley, in Surrey, in 1128. Rievaulx followed three years later. Melrose, in 1136, and Dundrennan, in Galloway, in 1142, were both established from there. Nine more Scottish Cistercian houses followed; the last, Sweetheart, in Galloway, as late as 1273.

The order set up its monasteries in remote places, 'far from the concourse of men'; its lands and industries were worked solely by and for the community. They achieved this by admitting lay brothers into its ranks, men who took the monastic vows and lived a cloistered life but who undertook a greater part of the manual labour at the expense of the religious life. They were permitted longer sleep and more food for their pains.

The monks and lay brothers wore undyed or white woollen habits and became commonly known as 'the white monks'. Beneath their habits they wore no undershirts or woollen breeches – not even in Scotland! Their diet was strictly vegetarian, but wholesome.

Above: Rievaulx Abbey, Yorkshire, the mother house of Melrose.

Left: A Cistercian or 'white' monk.

Right: A map showing the location of the Cistercian monasteries established in medieval Scotland.

1098

CISTERCIAN ORDER is founded at Citeaux, France, by Abbot Robert of Molesme. A very strict order, its monks rely on lay brothers to do all the manual work.

1136

MELROSE ABBEY is established by monks from Rievaulx, Yorkshire. Melrose becomes one of the biggest wool producers in Britain, with 15,000 sheep.

The Cistercian life was dedicated to prayer and physical work. It revolved daily around the eight 'hours' or church offices; the remainder of the day was divided by work, sleep or private prayer. The abbot at his head was assisted by other officers who supervised the various activities. These included the prior, his deputy, the precentor, who arranged the church services, the cellarer, who provisioned the cellars, and the almoner who looked after the poor. Links with the outside world were restricted to the abbot, who was frequently absent on state business, and the lay brethren, who staffed the granges (sheep farms).

Above: A cellarer takes a sneaky swig from the barrel.

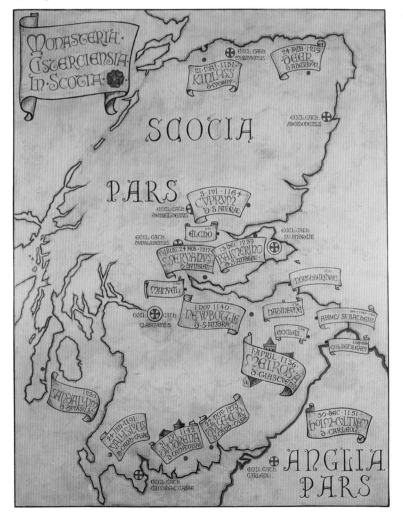

'Our food is scanty, our garments rough; our drink is from the stream and our sleep is often upon our book. Under our tired limbs there is but a hard mat; when sleep is sweetest we must rise at bell's bidding... Self will has no place; there is no moment for idleness or dissipation... Everywhere peace, everywhere serenity and a marvellous freedom from the tumult of the world.'

Abbot Aelred of Rievaulx (1147-67)

FOUNDATION

David I (1124–53) invited the Cistercians from Rievaulx Abbey, Yorkshire, to Melrose. He liberally endowed it, and encouraged others to do likewise. In this way the monks received land as far away as Ayrshire, property in towns such as Berwick and Edinburgh, and other assets in the form of fishing rights, salt-marshes and peat-bogs. Such was Melrose's popularity that it became one of Scotland's wealthiest monasteries. It was also held in great regard, and Robert Avenel, lord of Eskdale, and Richard de Moreville, high constable of Scotland, enrolled as novices there in the evening of their days.

David I's step-son, Waltheof, the second abbot, was renowned for performing miracles. Eleven years after his burial in the chapter house in 1159, his tomb was opened and his body found perfectly intact. Again in 1206, when a mason was working on a new tomb cover, he peeped inside and found it still complete. In 1240, a few small bones were removed as relics for pilgrims to touch and be cured. Remains from his shrine, found in 1921, are displayed in the commendator's house.

Above: A thirteenth-century tombstone found in the abbey.

Top left: King David I, from a charter of 1159 granted to Kelso Abbey.

Left: Fragments of St Waltheof's shrine, found in the chapter house in 1921.

1159

ST WALTHEOF

step-son of David I, founder of the abbey, and its second abbot, dies at Melrose. His tomb soon becomes a shrine for pilgrims.

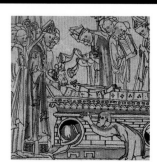

1249

KING ALEXANDER II

is buried in the abbey church, his body brought all the way from Argyll, where he died fighting the Norwegians.

THE FIRST CHURCH

The 13 monks arriving from Rievaulx (Abbot Richard and 12 others, signifying Christ and his disciples) began building their new abbey in strict accordance with the Rule of the order, first embarking on the east end of the abbey church. The work must have been sufficiently advanced by 1146 to enable the dedication service to take place. Building work continued for the next 50 years.

Little of the first church is now visible, but excavation has identified the main elements of the plan. It follows closely the original plan of Rievaulx, which in turn was probably modelled on Clairvaux, the Cistercians' house in eastern France from which Rievaulx was founded.

The church had a rectangular presbytery two bays long, flanked by two single-bay chapels and two transepts. Together they formed an unusual stepped arrangement at the east end. Beyond the crossing, the aisled nave stretched back for a further nine bays. The west door was later enclosed within a porch. The simplicity of the architecture for which the Cistercians were renowned at this date is evident in the surviving west wall (page 6-7).

'The church of St Mary, Malros, was dedicated upon the fifth of the kalends of June [28 June] being Sunday.'

An entry in the *Melrose Chronicle* 1146

Above: A monk at work on the *Melrose Chronicle*. The *Chronicle*, recording national events as well as events in the life of the monastery, was produced by a succession of monks from the time of the abbey's foundation until the late fourteenth century.

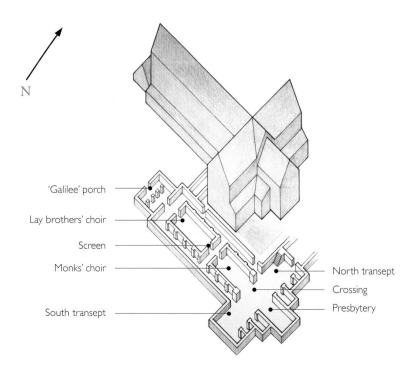

N

'Galilee' porch
Lay brothers' choir
Screen
Monks' choir
South transept
North transept
Crossing
Presbytery

Left: The arrangement of the first church.

MELROSE AND THE WARS WITH ENGLAND

The first 200 years passed peacefully enough, the only disruptions to the monastic routine being those imposed by the construction works and numerous land disputes. But this tranquil idyll was suddenly disrupted in 1296 with Edward I of England's invasion, and Melrose, at the heart of the Border country, was to suffer repeated depredations at the hands of the 'auld enemy' for the next 250 years.

Shortly after the outbreak of the wars with England, Abbot Patrick swore an oath of allegiance to the English king at Berwick, but his act brought little peace to the monastery. In 1322 Edward II's army sacked the abbey. King Robert the Bruce (1306-29) helped the monks rebuild it.

This devotion to Melrose received final recognition when, a month before he died, Bruce instructed that his heart be buried there. Some chroniclers, though, tell how, on his deathbed, Bruce made his friend, 'the Good Sir James of Douglas', swear to carry his heart on crusade, how Sir James fell fighting the Moors in Spain, and how, in 1331, Bruce's heart was returned to Scotland and buried in Melrose. (The king's body had earlier been interred in Dunfermline Abbey.)

Following David II's return to Scotland in 1357 from long imprisonment in England, an uneasy peace returned to the Borders. But in 1385 the Scots invaded England, and back came the English with a vengeance. Richard II's soldiers devastated the eastern Borders, and a chronicler bemoaned that they had 'burnt down with the fiery flames God's temples and holy places, to wit the monasteries of Melrose, Dryburgh and Newbattle'. The monks looked at their smoking ruin and decided there was nothing for it but to rebuild anew. Over the course of the next 100 years and more, the masons set about creating what is still one of the marvels of medieval church architecture anywhere in the British Isles. The quality of their craftsmanship is quite superb; the richness of the ornamentation awe-inspiring - in stark contrast with the plain lines and unadorned surfaces of its burned-down predecessor. The Cistercians had moved a long way from the simple aspirations of their founding fathers.

'...in the same monastery...one monk who was then sick and two blind lay brethren were killed in the dormitory by the English, and a great many more were wounded unto death. The Lord's Body was cast forth upon the High Altar and the pyx wherein it was kept taken away.'

An entry in the *Chronicle* recording the sack of Melrose by the army of Edward II of England in 1322.

Right: The magnificent presbytery and flanking transepts; painted by Robert Billings in 1832.

1331

1385

BRUCE'S HEART
is buried in the abbey
church following its return
from Spain. The king's body
had earlier been buried in
Dunfermline Abbey.

**RICHARD II
OF ENGLAND**
destroys the abbey church.
A new building rises from
the ashes.

A PHOENIX FROM THE ASHES

The rebuilding work began almost immediately within a year or two of the burning, probably under the aegis of Richard II who seems to have regarded southern Scotland as having been conquered. He certainly made financial provision for the work in 1389, and the architectural evidence supports the belief that part at least of 'the new werke of thaine kirke of Melros' was carried out by English masons. The clue is in the windows of the new presbytery, where the tracery is mostly in the English 'perpendicular' style; their nearest parallels are in eastern England, as at Beverley St Mary in Yorkshire. That responsibility for the building work passed after a while to masons from another tradition is also evident in the fabric for there is a distinct change in style, most obviously in the south transept and the south aisle chapels. Here the more flowing window tracery has been inspired by European buildings, and two inscriptions in the south transept record that this particular part of the work was supervised by the French master-mason, John Morow (page 12).

The rebuilding work continued through the fifteenth and into the sixteenth century; James IV distributed drink-silver to the masons during his visits in 1502 and 1504. The church was probably never actually completed, but even in its unfinished state it must have been magnificent to behold. Today's visitor has only the splendour of the masonry to admire, with its exquisite, captivating and humorous carvings. The pretty rose-tinted sandstone was quarried from the neighbouring Eildon Hills. The glazed floor tiles, coloured yellow, green or brown and set in geometric patterns, can be seen on display in the commendator's house. Alas, of the monks' choir stalls, ordered from Cornelius de Aeltre of Bruges in the 1430s, nothing at all remains.

Above: The more flowing window tracery in the south transept suggests that by the time building work reached here the original English masons had been replaced by others influenced by French fashion.

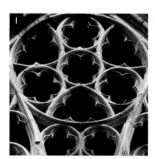

Left:

1 A window in the south aisle chapel.

2 The vaulted ceiling above the high altar.

3 The crossing tower and north transept.

DECLINE AND FALL

Little is known of the day-to-day story of Melrose as the Middle Ages wore on, but what is clear is that it was not only the church architecture that was changing. The economy continued to revolve around the sale of high-quality wool, but was now produced on tenanted farms rather than on granges run by the lay brothers, who had probably disappeared by 1443 when their former choir in the nave was adapted for parish worship. The abbots were also taking on roles different to those expected of them by their founder. Now, as statesmen and courtiers, they were frequently absent from the cloister, leaving control of the monastery to their priors. Abbot Andrew Hunter, for example, was James II's treasurer in 1450.

The dilution of the strict Cistercian Rule, even for the monks, is evident in a ruling made by the abbots of Coupar Angus and Glenluce who decreed in 1534 that the practice at Melrose of allowing individual monks to have private lodgings and gardens must cease on pain of excommunication. A dispensation was permitted for the gardens to continue as long as the produce was for the good of the whole community.

One sign of the decline was the appointment in 1541 of James V's eldest son, James Stewart, as commendator, or administrator of the monastery and the enforced resignation of the last abbot, Andrew Durie. James was an infant at the time!

'the monks of melrose made gude kail on fridays when they fasted; nor wanted they gude beef and ale, as lang's their neighbour's lasted.'

From an old Border ballad hinting at the relaxed nature of monastic life at the time of the Reformation.

Above:
Abbot Hunter's tower at Mauchline provided a comfortable lodging for him on his occasional visits to the abbey's Ayrshire estates.

1400

JOHN MOROW
A French master mason, creates the stunning south transept and eastern aisle chapels.

1541

ABBOT ANDREW DURIE
resigns as abbot of Melrose (1524-41). He is replaced by a non-monastic administrator.

THE END OF AN ERA

Abbot Durie resigned just in time to avoid the full horrors of war. James V's death in 1542, and the accession of his daughter Mary to the throne, led to the 'War of the Rough Wooing', so-called because of Henry VIII's violent attempts to persuade the Scots to let Mary marry his son Edward. In 1544 the English set fire to the abbey church and desecrated the tombs. They returned in the following year. Ironically, Sir Ralph Evers, the English commander killed at the nearby battle of Ancrum Moor, was buried in the very church he himself had looted the previous year!

The few remaining monks tried to persuade the commendator to repair their cloister, but in vain. In 1556 they warned that 'without the kirk be repairit this instant sommer God service will ceise this winter'. Four years later, the Protestant Reformation brought their form of 'God service' to an end.

'...without the kirk be repairit this instant sommer God service will ceise this winter.'

A complaint lodged by the sub-prior and three monks against the commendator in 1556.

Below: The monastery precinct c1500; an impression by Alan Sorrell.

Just how many monks were in residence in 1560 is not known; in 1539 the number was down to 22, including the abbot and prior. Desirous of retaining their 'private pensions', they renounced monasticism and embraced the reformed religion. But the buildings were falling down about their ears. In 1573 Sir Walter Scott of Branxholm was accused by them of dismantling 'the inner queir' [the monks' choir], the 'uter kirk' [the nave], 'the stepile and croce kirk of the same' [the tower and transepts] and carrying off the stones, timber, lead, iron and glass and later of taking away similar materials from the abbot's hall. His excuse? He was only removing the materials to save them from falling into the hands of the English!

Soon after 1590 Dan Jo Watson, who had shortly before signed himself as 'only convent', passed away. The story of almost 1000 years of monasticism at Melrose died with him.

Dan Jo Watson's death was not quite the end of the story though. The crumbling abbey church continued to be used by the townsfolk and about 1610 part of the former monks' choir was converted for parochial use and a belfry was erected at the top of the south transept gable. Part of the ruined cloister was retained by the last commendator, James Douglas, and converted into an acceptable residence. When that headstrong nobleman was executed, the abbey lands were sold by the Crown in small lots to various nobles. The lordship of Melrose went to the earls of Haddington, and from them it was bought by Anne, duchess of Buccleuch, widow of the ill-fated Monmouth. With the erection in 1810 of a new parish kirk on the Weirhill, elsewhere in the town, the story of Melrose Abbey finally came to a close.

'If thou would'st view fair melrose aright,

go visit it by pale moonlight;

for the gay beams of lightsome day

gild, but to flount the ruins grey.'

Sir Walter Scott
Lay of the Last Minstrel 1805

1590

1810

DAN JO WATSON
Melrose's last Cistercian monk, dies. Monastic life formally comes to an end.

NEW PARISH KIRK
built on the Weirhill. The ruined abbey is preserved as an ancient monument.

Melrose Abbey is one of 12 Historic Scotland sites situated in the Scottish Borders. (A selection of these sites is shown below.) For more information visit: **www.historic-scotland.gov.uk**

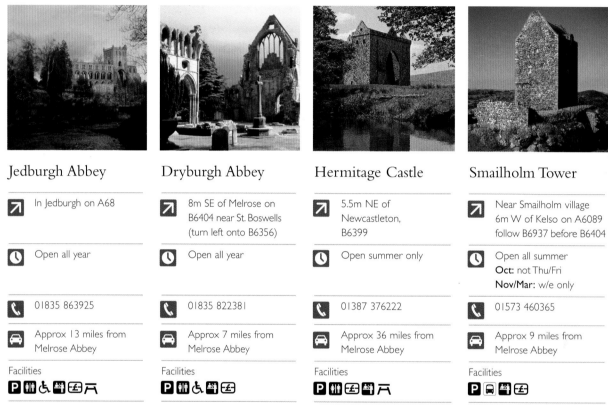

Jedburgh Abbey

↗ In Jedburgh on A68

🕐 Open all year

📞 01835 863925

🚗 Approx 13 miles from Melrose Abbey

Facilities

Dryburgh Abbey

↗ 8m SE of Melrose on B6404 near St. Boswells (turn left onto B6356)

🕐 Open all year

📞 01835 822381

🚗 Approx 7 miles from Melrose Abbey

Facilities

Hermitage Castle

↗ 5.5m NE of Newcastleton, B6399

🕐 Open summer only

📞 01387 376222

🚗 Approx 36 miles from Melrose Abbey

Facilities

Smailholm Tower

↗ Near Smailholm village 6m W of Kelso on A6089 follow B6937 before B6404

🕐 Open all summer **Oct:** not Thu/Fri **Nov/Mar:** w/e only

📞 01573 460365

🚗 Approx 9 miles from Melrose Abbey

Facilities

Why not visit our online shop: Tickets to all Historic Scotland monuments and a wide range of products, including guidebooks and souvenirs, can be ordered online at www.historic-scotland.gov.uk/shop

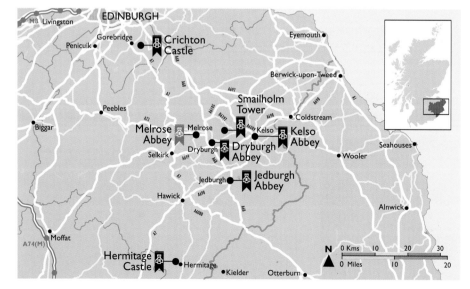

Facilities (Key)

Admission charge	💷
Bus/coach parking	🚌
Car parking	🅿
Interpretive display	🚩
Picnic area	⛉
Reasonable wheelchair access	♿
Shop	🛍
Toilets	🚻

NB: Strong footwear is recommended for visitors to Crichton Castle and Smailholm Tower.